The Climate Crisis

OCEANS, GLACIERS, AND RISING SEA LEVELS

A Graphic Guide

Christina Hill
illustrated by Julie Lerche

Graphic Universe™ • Minneapolis

Graphic Universe™
An imprint of Lerner Publishing Group, Inc.
241 First Avenue North
Minneapolis, MN 55401 USA

For reading levels and more information, look up this title at www.lernerbooks.com.

Main body text is set in Dave Gibbons Lower. Typeface provided by Comicraft.

Library of Congress Cataloging-in-Publication Data

Names: Hill, Christina, author. | Lerche, Julie, illustrator.
Title: Oceans, glaciers, and rising sea levels : a graphic guide / written by Christina Hill ; illustrated by Julie Lerche.
Description: Minneapolis : Graphic Universe, [2023] | Series: The climate crisis | Includes bibliographical references and index. | Audience: Ages 8–12 | Audience: Grades 4–6 | Summary: "As our planet warms, glaciers are melting faster than usual. Sea levels rise, and water washes over coastal areas. Discover the changes humans need to make to keep our heads above water"— Provided by publisher.
Identifiers: LCCN 2023009725 (print) | LCCN 2023009726 (ebook) | ISBN 9781728476889 (library binding) | ISBN 9798765623510 (paperback) | ISBN 9798765613276 (epub)
Subjects: LCSH: Glaciers—Pictorial works—Juvenile literature. | Global warming—Pictorial works—Juvenile literature. | Climatic changes—Pictorial works—Juvenile literature. | BISAC: JUVENILE NONFICTION / Science & Nature / Earth Sciences / Water (Oceans, Lakes, etc.)
Classification: LCC GB2403.8 .H55 2023 (print) | LCC GB2403.8 (ebook) | DDC 551.45/8—dc23/eng20230624

LC record available at https://lccn.loc.gov/2023009725
LC ebook record available at https://lccn.loc.gov/2023009726

Manufactured in the United States of America
1 – CG – 7/15/23

TABLE OF CONTENTS

Chapter One: Glaciers Over Time

Earth looked very different from this scene when it formed 4.5 billion years ago. Its surface was once completely covered in water. The continents were connected, forming one supercontinent. Over time, Earth's landscape changed. It is still changing.

Glaciers form when snow remains on land and doesn't melt. The snow becomes tightly packed and dense. Over time, a large ice mass forms.

Seventy percent of Earth is made up of water. About 2.5 percent of that water is freshwater. Nearly 75 percent of that freshwater is frozen in glaciers.

Glaciers are found all over Earth, but mostly at its poles. Antarctica is home to 91 percent of glaciers. Around 8 percent are on the opposite side of the globe, in Greenland. The high snowfall and the cooler summers at Earth's poles mean less of the snow melts.

Glaciers are important for many communities. The small amounts of glacier ice that naturally melt during warmer months provide people with fresh drinking water.

Scientists who study glaciers are called glaciologists. They have seen that some glaciers are melting and disappearing at an increasing rate. This is called glacier retreat.

Scientists have determined that glaciers are melting at a faster rate due to an increase in average temperatures around the world.

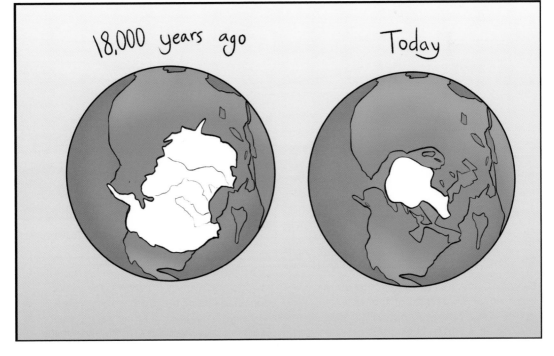

Gases make up Earth's atmosphere. As the sun shines on Earth, some of these gases trap heat. The trapped heat warms the air and provides temperatures that sustain plant and animal life.

During the 20th century, the average global temperature on Earth was 57°F (13.9°C).

But Earth's average temperature, or climate, has changed over time. As the climate changes, Earth's landscapes and ecosystems change too.

When dinosaurs lived, there were no ice caps at the poles.

Modern glaciers formed from ice sheets left from the last ice age, around 20,000 years ago.

Most of North America was covered in giant ice sheets. But the average global temperature was 47°F (8.3°C), only 10°F (5°C) colder than the average temperatures in the 20th century.

Just a few degrees of change in average global temperature greatly affects the planet. Some experts say we need to limit global warming to below 2.7°F (1.5°C). If we exceed that, there will be extreme changes that we can't stop. This is called reaching the tipping point.

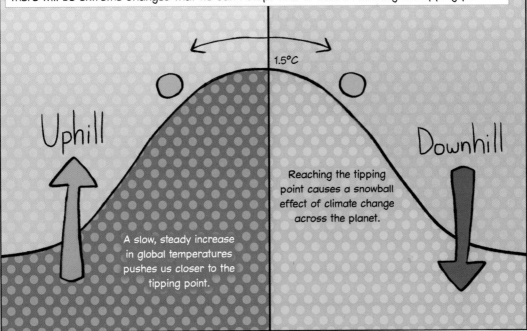

1.5°C

Uphill

Downhill

A slow, steady increase in global temperatures pushes us closer to the tipping point.

Reaching the tipping point causes a snowball effect of climate change across the planet.

The way Earth's atmosphere traps heat is called the greenhouse effect. Without it, Earth's temperature would be −243°F (−153°C).

The planet's atmosphere is mostly made up of oxygen and nitrogen. These gases cannot absorb heat. But other gases, such as carbon dioxide, do trap heat in the atmosphere. This led to the name *greenhouse* gases.

Scientists link these gases to the current period of global warming.

It appears the global warming trend started in the early 1800s. Look at the increase in carbon dioxide in the air.

Ocean surface temperatures are also warming.

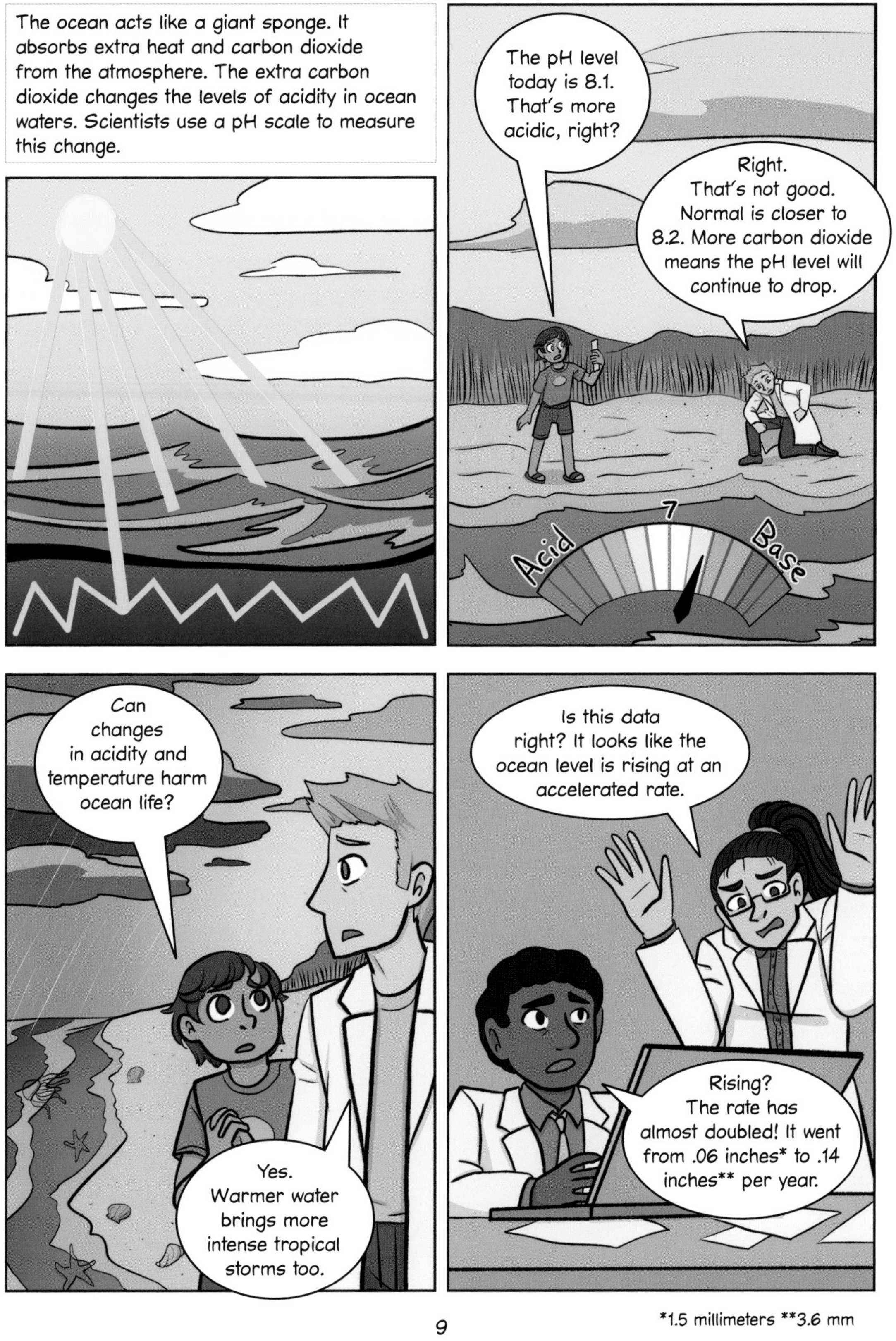
The ocean acts like a giant sponge. It absorbs extra heat and carbon dioxide from the atmosphere. The extra carbon dioxide changes the levels of acidity in ocean waters. Scientists use a pH scale to measure this change.
The pH level today is 8.1. That's more acidic, right?
Right. That's not good. Normal is closer to 8.2. More carbon dioxide means the pH level will continue to drop.
Acid
7
Base
Can changes in acidity and temperature harm ocean life?
Yes. Warmer water brings more intense tropical storms too.
Is this data right? It looks like the ocean level is rising at an accelerated rate.
Rising? The rate has almost doubled! It went from .06 inches* to .14 inches** per year.

*1.5 millimeters **3.6 mm

The main cause of rising sea levels is the melting of glaciers. When this happens, the freshwater runs into the oceans.

As ocean levels rise, more water covers shorelines. Beaches disappear. Coastal wildlife habitats such as marshes and wetlands are flooded.

Thermal expansion is another cause of changing sea levels. As water's temperature rises, the volume of the water increases and expands. The ocean water takes up more space, and the sea level rises too.

*22.86 centimeters

During the 1850s, Eunice Newton Foote explored the effects of the sun on different gases in the atmosphere.

Foote designed a homemade experiment with two glass cylinders, thermometers, and an air pump. One glass cylinder contained fresh air, and the other contained carbon dioxide. She discovered that the cylinder with carbon dioxide trapped more heat and stayed hot longer when it was in the sun.

The highest effect of the sun's rays I have found to be in carbon dioxide. An atmosphere of that gas would give our Earth a high temperature.

In 1856, Foote's paper "Circumstances Affecting the Heat of the Sun's Rays" was presented at the American Association for the Advancement of Science. Joseph Henry, director of the Smithsonian, presented the paper for her.

At the time, male scientists did not recognize women's efforts. It was years before Foote's observations were taken seriously.

Climate change is a natural occurrence that has happened throughout history. There does not appear to be any cause for alarm.

Despite the work of Foote and others, the general public didn't know much about greenhouse gases and climate change. But this all changed in 1988.

In 1988, Dr. James Hansen, director of the NASA Goddard Institute for Space Studies, testified to the US Congress.

Global warming is now large enough that we can ascribe with a high degree of confidence a cause-and-effect relationship to the greenhouse effect. ... it is changing our climate now.

Hansen's testimony was a call to action. Global warming was a problem that needed to be addressed. Human activity was to blame for the added greenhouse gases.

People were letting more greenhouse gases into the atmosphere through factories, cars, and the cutting down of trees.

Hansen's work helped explain events that people were already seeing. Increased flooding, melting ice sheets, rising sea levels, strong storms, and changes in ecosystems were directly related to global warming.

Hansen and other researchers began to focus on the effects of climate change. NASA satellites took photos from space to monitor changes in the thickness of glacier ice. These photos help scientists see any glacier retreat.

Climate scientists continue to study sections of ice to learn more about Earth's climate history. It also helps them make predictions for the future.

We can drill nearly 1 mile* into the polar ice sheet. The large chunk of ice that we remove is called an ice core. This ice core holds a record of years of climate data.

*1.6 kilometers

Each layer of ice contains particles that were present in the atmosphere at the time the snow fell. This gives scientists clues about events that happened in the past. The oldest ice core samples are 800,000 years old.

Look at the ash in this ice. There was a volcanic eruption around this time.

The bubbles of gas trapped in the ice can tell us if the levels of greenhouse gases changed.

The ice cores are packed and stored here. We can borrow samples if we need them for research.

Ice core samples and satellite pictures help scientists understand climate change and its effect on glaciers.

Rising water levels can tell us about climate change. But Earth's sea levels vary in different regions, so it is difficult to measure sea level rise. Satellites have helped solve this problem. A satellite sends a radar signal down to the ocean's surface and calculates the distance.

Scientists subtract the distance between the satellite and the ocean's surface from the distance between the satellite and Earth's core. This gives them the measure of the distance between Earth's core and the surface of the ocean.

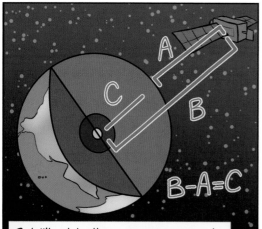

Satellites take the same measurements across Earth. This data gives scientists an accurate average sea level.

Researchers also place buoys throughout the ocean to record the amount of carbon dioxide in the water. This way, they can measure pH levels.

Special robots called Argo floats dive deep into the ocean. They record water temperatures at different depths. They are able to see how ocean heat moves through the water.

Between 2002 and 2017, the Gravity Recovery and Climate Experiment (GRACE) satellites measured small changes in Earth's gravity from the melting glacier water. They took measurements to see how gravity affects the way water moves on Earth.

The satellites show that melting glacier ice and excess rainfall are flowing to the ocean.

Sea levels in 2020 were 3.6 inches* above the 1993 levels. This is severe!

GLOBAL SEA LEVEL

*9.1 cm

Chapter Three: Extreme Effects

Dr. Jennifer Francis is a scientist in Massachusetts who studies the impact of rising sea levels.

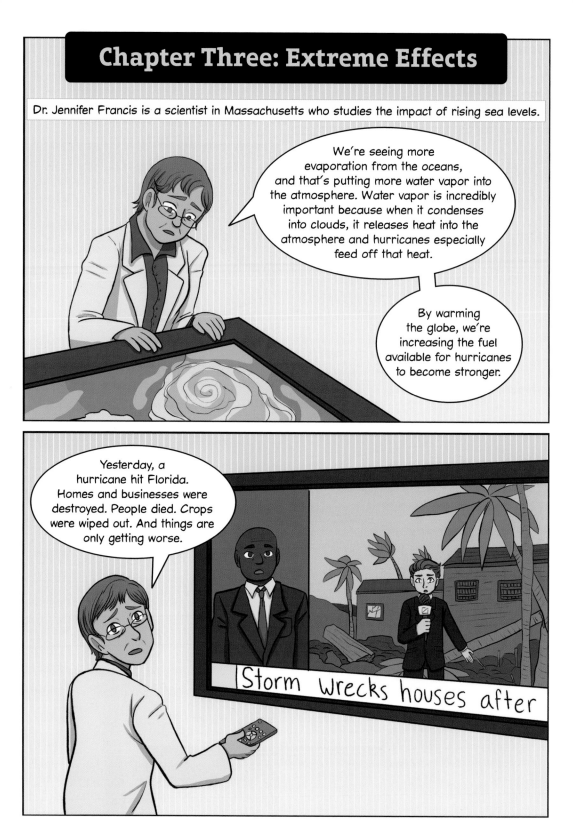

We're seeing more evaporation from the oceans, and that's putting more water vapor into the atmosphere. Water vapor is incredibly important because when it condenses into clouds, it releases heat into the atmosphere and hurricanes especially feed off that heat.

By warming the globe, we're increasing the fuel available for hurricanes to become stronger.

Yesterday, a hurricane hit Florida. Homes and businesses were destroyed. People died. Crops were wiped out. And things are only getting worse.

Storm wrecks houses after

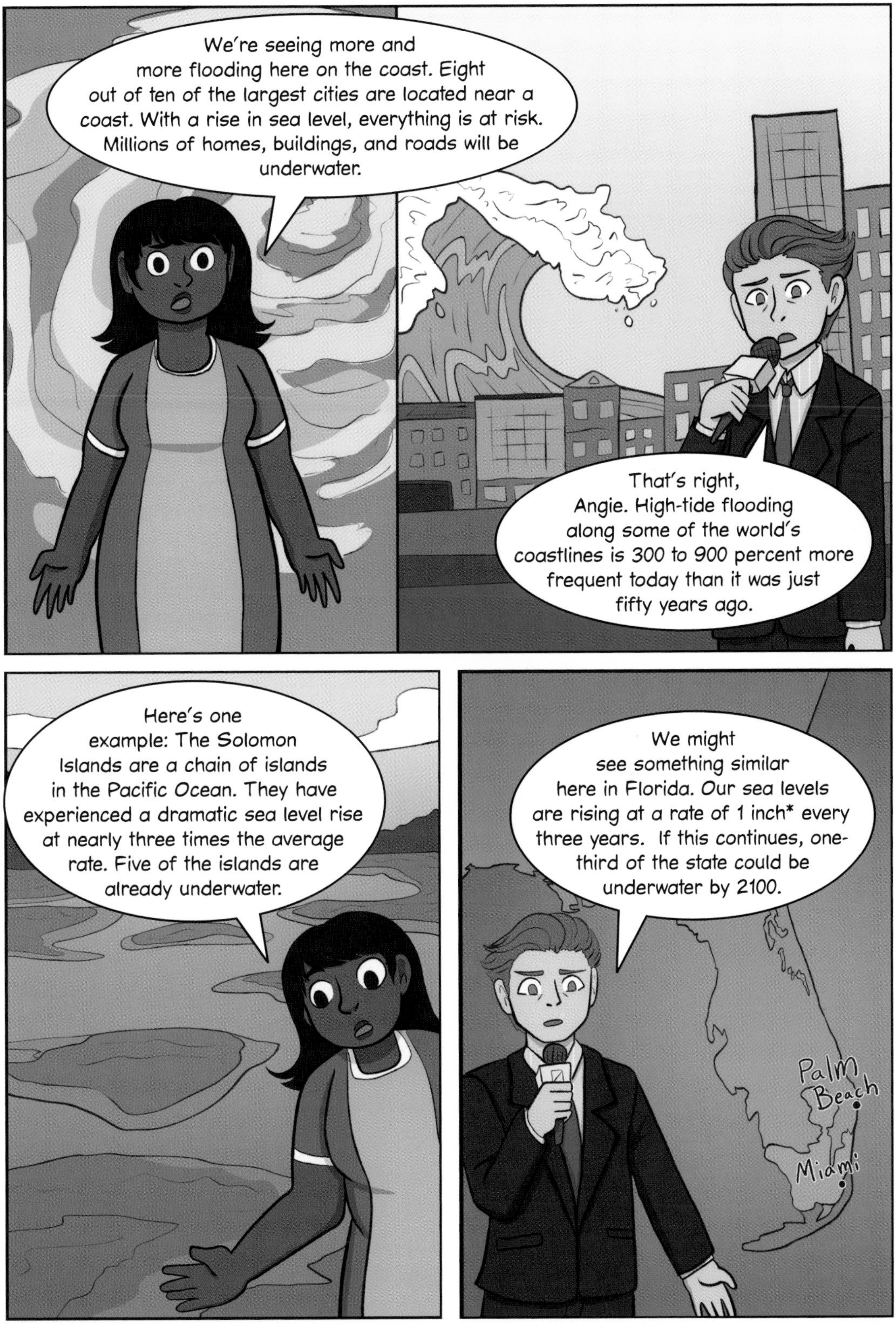
We're seeing more and more flooding here on the coast. Eight out of ten of the largest cities are located near a coast. With a rise in sea level, everything is at risk. Millions of homes, buildings, and roads will be underwater.
That's right, Angie. High-tide flooding along some of the world's coastlines is 300 to 900 percent more frequent today than it was just fifty years ago.
Here's one example: The Solomon Islands are a chain of islands in the Pacific Ocean. They have experienced a dramatic sea level rise at nearly three times the average rate. Five of the islands are already underwater.
We might see something similar here in Florida. Our sea levels are rising at a rate of 1 inch* every three years. If this continues, one-third of the state could be underwater by 2100.
Palm Beach
Miami

*2.5 cm

As the sea level rises along a coastline, water begins to cover more land. Birds, plants, and animals need coastal marshes to survive, but these areas will become flooded.

Nearly 90 percent of coastal freshwater turtles will be at risk from the increase in saltwater and lack of freshwater. As sea levels rise, beach habitats are washed away. Sea turtles will lose the shoreline they use to lay their eggs.

As the ocean absorbs more carbon dioxide, it becomes more acidic. Warmer and more acidic ocean waters are hurting fish populations. There is less oxygen in the water for fish to breathe. There are fewer places for fish to spawn.

Ice that melts, and covers land with water, causes losses for animals too. Polar bears use sea ice as their main habitat. They stand on the ice when they hunt for seals. The loss of ice means they have to travel to find food.

Sea ice provides walruses with a place to rest. As the ice melts, they are forced onto shore, where it is hard for them to survive.

Warmer ocean water is also causing stress to coral reefs. Protective and colorful algae cover the coral and serve as its food source. The algae disappear when the coral is stressed.

Scientists are discovering that acidic waters are causing clown fish to stray far away from the safety of their reef homes. In the open water, they fall victim to predators.

Some marine life, such as oysters and snails, are losing their shells because of low pH.

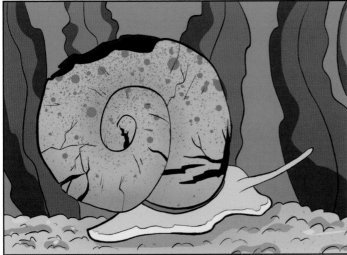

Tiny sea snails are an important food source for birds and fish. The calcium found in snail shells is a needed nutrient. Snails without shells are weaker and easier for predators to catch. If their life cycles end sooner than expected, the population won't survive. This one change affects the entire food chain. The percentage of snails with dissolved shells is set to triple by 2050.

Another poor day of fishing. Seems like most fish have left, looking for cooler water and more food. I can't last much longer on catches like this either.

Chapter Four: Hope for the Future

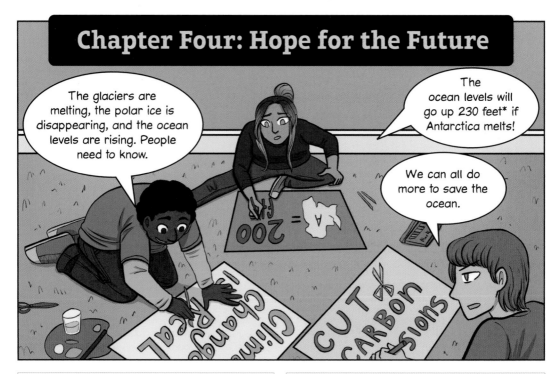

In 2016, many countries around the world signed the Paris Agreement. The goal of this agreement is to keep the global temperature rise to below 3.6°F (−15.8°C) by reducing greenhouse gases.

The US first joined the Paris Agreement in 2016 but withdrew in 2020. President Joe Biden re-signed the treaty on his first day in office in 2021.

Support from the government is essential in fighting climate change. Gina McCarthy works as the White House National Climate Advisor.

We must redouble our efforts to cut the greenhouse gases that cause climate change while, at the same time, help our coastal communities become more resilient in the face of rising seas.

If nothing changes and all of the glaciers and polar ice melt, global sea level will rise 230 feet. Nearly every coastal city would be completely underwater.

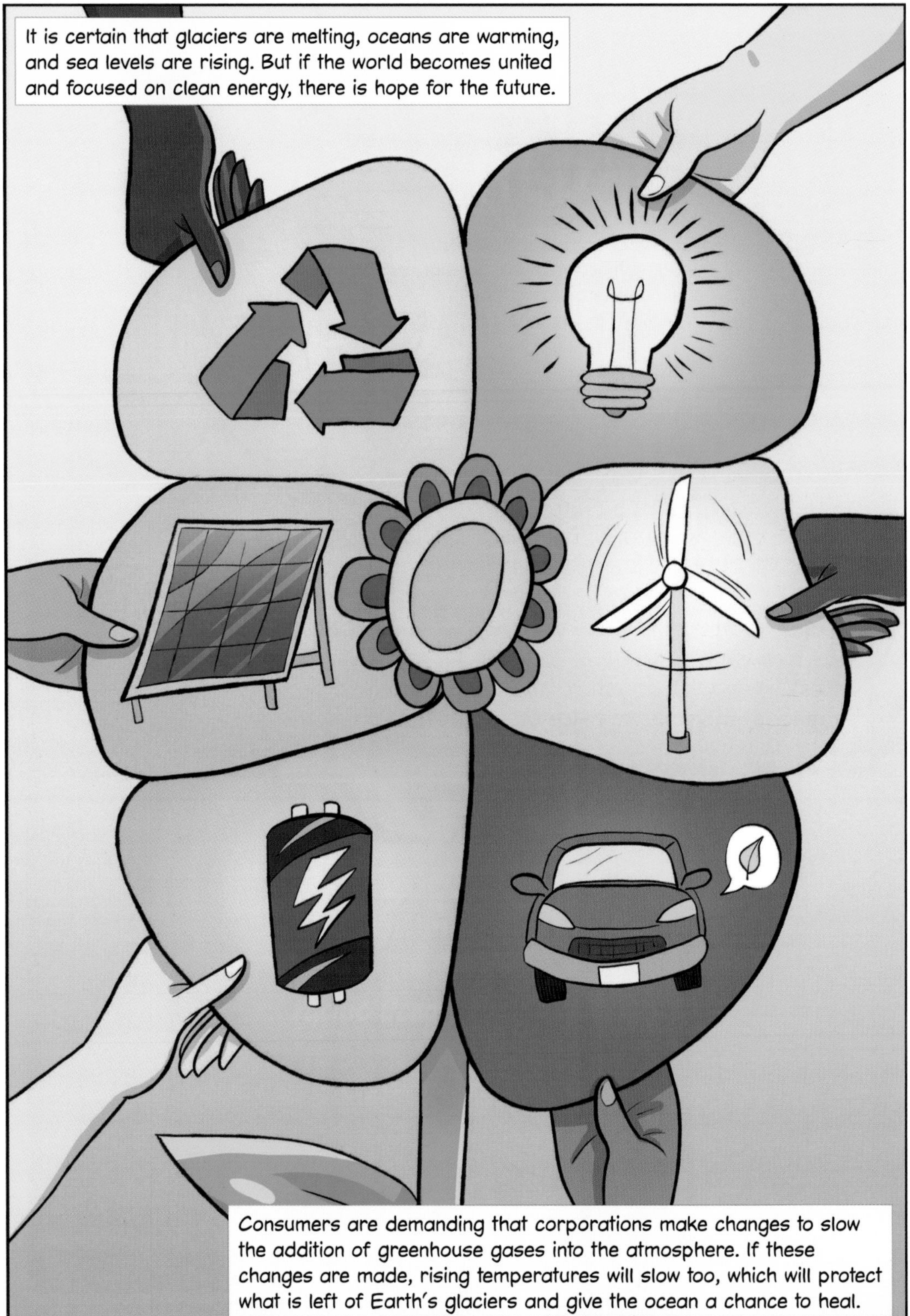
It is certain that glaciers are melting, oceans are warming, and sea levels are rising. But if the world becomes united and focused on clean energy, there is hope for the future.
Consumers are demanding that corporations make changes to slow the addition of greenhouse gases into the atmosphere. If these changes are made, rising temperatures will slow too, which will protect what is left of Earth's glaciers and give the ocean a chance to heal.

SOURCE NOTES

12 Elisha Foote, *On the Heat in the Sun's Rays (American Journal of Science and Arts)*, 383.

14 "Congressional Testimony of Dr. James Hansen," SeaLevel.info, June 23, 1988, https://www.sealevel.info/1988_Hansen_Senate_Testimony.html

15 Dr. James E. Hansen, "James Hansen: Why I Must Speak Out About Climate Change," *TED*, March 7, 2012, https://www.youtube.com /watch?v=fWInyaMWBY8

20 Chris Remington, "Researcher Examines Impact of Melting Polar Ice On Hurricanes," *WLRN Public Radio and Television*, April 30, 2019, https://www.wlrn.org/show/sundial/2019-04-30/researcher-examines -impact-of-melting-polar-ice-on-hurricanes

GLOSSARY

atmosphere: the mass of air that surrounds a planet

carbon dioxide: gas that is produced when certain fuels are burned

ecosystems: plants, animals, and elements that exist in a particular environment

evaporation: the change from a liquid to a gas

fossil fuels: coal, oil, or natural gas that is formed in Earth

glaciers: large areas of ice

glaciologists: scientists who study glaciers

greenhouse effect: gases that trap heat in Earth's atmosphere like a greenhouse

habitat: the natural place where a plant or animal lives

NASA: the National Aeronautics and Space Administration

pH scale: the scale used to determine if something is a base, neutral, or acid

radar: a sensor that uses radio waves to find or track objects

spawn: to deposit eggs into the water

thermal expansion: the increase in an object's volume because of a rise in temperature. When temperatures rise, objects expand. When temperatures cool, objects contract or shrink.

variation: the amount of change

FURTHER READING

Britannica Kids: Global Warming
https://kids.britannica.com/students/article/global-warming/311438

Ducksters: Glaciers
https://www.ducksters.com/science/earth_science/glaciers.php

Henzel, Cynthia Kennedy. *Redesigning Cities to Fight Climate Change.* Lake Elmo, MN: Focus Readers, 2023.

Klein, Naomi. *How to Change Everything: The Young Human's Guide to Protecting the Planet and Each Other.* New York: Atheneum Books for Young Readers, 2021.

Kurtz, Kevin. *Climate Change and Rising Temperatures.* Minneapolis: Lerner Publications, 2019.

TED Talk: James Hansen
https://www.ted.com/talks/james_hansen_why_i_must_speak_out_about_climate_change?language=en

INDEX